GETTING HIRED

A Guide for Managers and Professionals

Richard J. Pinsker, CMC

A FIFTY-MINUTE™ SERIES BOOK

CRISP PUBLICATIONS, INC.
Menlo Park, California

GETTING HIRED

A Guide for Managers and Professionals

Richard J. Pinsker, CMC

CREDITS:
Editor: **Andrea Reider**
Typesetting: **ExecuStaff**
Cover Design: **Carol Harris**
Artwork: **Ralph Mapson**

Printed in the United States of America by Bawden Printing Company.

English language Crisp books are distributed worldwide. Our major international distributors include:

CANADA: Reid Publishing, Ltd., Box 69559—109 Thomas St., Oakville, Ontario Canada L6J 7R4. TEL: (416) 842-4428, FAX: (416) 842-9327

AUSTRALIA: Career Builders, P.O. Box 1051, Springwood, Brisbane, Queensland, Australia 4127. TEL: 841-1061, FAX: 841-1580

NEW ZEALAND: Career Builders, P.O. Box 571, Manurewa, Auckland, New Zealand. TEL: 266-5276, FAX: 266-4152

JAPAN: Phoenix Associates Co., Mizuho Bldg. 2-12-2, Kami Osaki, Shinagawa-Ku, Tokyo 141, Japan. TEL: 3-443-7231, FAX: 3-443-7640

Selected Crisp titles are also available in other languages. Contact International Rights Manager Suzanne Kelly at (415) 323-6100 for more information.

Library of Congress Catalog Card Number 93-73202
Pinsker, Richard J.
Getting Hired
ISBN 1-56052-252-6

This book is printed on recyclable paper with soy ink.

ABOUT THIS BOOK

Getting Hired is not like most books. It has a unique ''self-study'' format that encourages a reader to become personally involved. Designed to be ''read with a pencil,'' there are exercises, activities, assessments and cases that invite participation.

Whether you are a career newcomer, a professional in transition, or someone interested in future career advancement, you will find this book invaluable as an action-planning guide. You can use the ideas in *Getting Hired* throughout your career to ensure maximum job opportunity exposure.

Getting Hired can be used effectively in a number of ways. Here are some possibilities:

- **Individual Study.** Because the book is self-instructional, all that is needed is a quiet place, some time and a pencil. Completing the activities and exercises will provide valuable feedback, as well as practical ideas for getting the job you want.
- **Workshops and Seminars.** This book is ideal for use during, or as pre-assigned reading prior to, a workshop or seminar. With the basics in hand, the quality of participation will improve. More time can be spent practicing concept extensions and applications during the program.
- **College Programs.** Thanks to the format, brevity and low cost, this book is ideal for short courses and extension programs.

There are other possibilities that depend on the objectives of the user. One thing is certain: even after it has been read, this book will serve as excellent reference material that can be easily reviewed.

ABOUT THE AUTHOR

Richard J. Pinsker is president of Pinsker and Company, an executive selection consulting firm. Through retained search engagements and executive selection workshops, his clients attract and hire the best executives, managers and professionals. He is a Certified Management Consultant and holds BS and MS degrees in psychology.

Dick has been a guest speaker on nationally syndicated talk shows, and at trade and professional associations. His articles on executive selection have appeared throughout the United States and England. He is the author of the Business Week Book Club Main Selection, *Hiring Winners,* (AMACOM, 1991), now in its second printing.

For information on Dick's executive selection consulting practice or to discuss a speaking engagement, please write to him at:

P.O. Box 3269
Saratoga, California 95070
Phone (408) 867-5161

PREFACE

Whether you have recently entered your career, are currently in the job market, or plan to make a managerial or professional job change, *Getting Hired* will make your search easier.

Do you know:

✓ Where and how companies find managers and professionals?

✓ How to reach the hiring decision makers?

✓ What you must include and exclude in your resume and cover letter?

✓ How "not" to respond to an employment advertisement?

✓ How to create a positive interview impression?

✓ How to use "between job consulting" to obtain a full-time position?

✓ What continual efforts are necessary to ensure more job opportunities?

The information in this book will give you the methods and techniques that companies and search firms use to find and evaluate candidates. You will learn where to be, how to get there, and what to expect.

Richard J. Pinsker

ACKNOWLEDGMENTS

Thanks to the hundreds of thousands of executives who unknowingly contributed their resumes to this book.

My appreciation to the hiring and human resources managers, and my consultant colleagues whose comments and advice have helped crystalize some of the ideas.

A special thanks to my wife Ginny for her continued support.

Dedicated to their futures:

Melinda, James, Jeffrey, Corey, Trevor and Matthew

KNOWING

By twenty we know we can do anything.

By thirty we know what we want to do.

By forty we know what we will do.

By fifty we know what we can do.

By sixty we know what we have done.

By seventy we know we could have done anything
but know we did our best.

—R. J. Pinsker

CONTENTS

CONTENTS (continued)

INTRODUCTION

There is a disturbing trend for many people in white collar jobs today. For the first time, professional and managerial workers are being laid-off in large numbers.

The downsizing of companies, perhaps once thought of as a temporary recessionary move, may be permanent. Companies in every industry continue to look for ways to reduce employment, while maintaining or increasing productivity. Thus, many jobs that are eliminated in downsizing are gone forever from the available positions list.

In this lean-and-mean approach to organization, companies are taking a very selective approach to hiring executives, managers and professionals. They are using extensive resources to identify winners. They are adopting the techniques of headhunters in-house to find suitable candidates. They are

- Reviewing more resumes
- Conducting more interviews
- Checking references more thoroughly
- Pursuing candidates with demonstrated bottom-line results

What does this mean to the executive, manager or professional who is without a job? What should you be doing now to insure your professional career?

Being in the *right place at the right time,* with the *right credentials,* will get you that job *almost every time!*

P A R T

1

Networking: Being in the Right Place at the Right Time

WHY NETWORK?

Networking is an ongoing process of letting the right people know who you are. Networking is being in the right place at the right time. Because it is so important *throughout your career,* we need to examine what networking is and how you can make it work to your advantage.

It's Who You Know

Opportunities for job changes do not just happen. Rather, they occur as a result of networking and job performance. The more extensive your network, the more career opportunities will be presented to you. Likewise, the greater the recognition of your job performance is, the more you will hear about available jobs.

Extensive Network	+	Good Job Performance	=	Job Opportunities

A young attorney joining a major law firm was given the following excellent advice:

- **Attend Seminars and Meetings**
- **Write Articles**
- **Speak Up**
- **Make Yourself Known**

And, of course, do a first class job. This is great advice for anyone at any point in their career.

Networking means being in front of people who represent the right place. These people can recommend, influence or make a hiring decision. But how do these influencers and decision makers get to know or hear about you? How can you be recognized as someone they should approach about a job?

HOW TO BE THE RESULT OF A RECRUITMENT EFFORT

Companies and recruitment firms look toward many sources to identify candidates for positions that they are seeking to fill. The impersonal approaches, such as advertisement responses, will be discussed later. However, the following is a list of sources that you should be pursuing and in contact with throughout your career. They become a top priority when you are in the job market.

Job Resource Checklist

In the box before each source, indicate the level of your activities or appropriateness.

C = Currently using source to its fullest

N = Need to use

P = Plan to use

I = Inappropriate for my career

☐ *Alumni Placement Offices*

A company will often call the alumni placement office of schools that they have determined may have the type of graduates that will fit their requirements. This is usually based on employees who have previously graduated from those schools. Make sure that the placement office has a current copy of your resume. Get to know the placement staff at each of the universities where you have received a degree.

☐ *Trade and Professional Associations*

These represent excellent opportunities for networking contacts. This activity is a must for anyone seeking a job change. Network with members at meetings. Take an active role as an officer or on a program. Provide an article for their publication. Keep a resume with their placement chairperson. Get noticed and remembered.

☐ *Bankers*

Your banker has many contacts in the community. Take the time to meet the top officers in your bank, especially if it is a small community or business bank. Let them know what you do and what you might be looking for in a career. These people often hear before the general public about companies on the verge of expanding.

☐ ***Business and Technical Articles***

Create the opportunity to be published. Note newspaper and magazine articles that you could have written, and submit articles to those publications. Concentrate on publications that are read by people that you want to influence.

☐ ***Competitors***

Competitors of your present company represent employers who may also have an interest in you. Know your competition. Whenever you have the opportunity, meet colleagues from other companies and establish communication links. If you are in the job market, let them know. Trade shows are an excellent place to meet your competitors.

☐ ***Community Groups and Affairs***

Take an active role in groups such as the Rotary Club, community fund raisers, and charitable events. It's a chance to rub elbows with the community movers and shakers who usually lead these efforts. Like you, they are volunteers from other organizations and may be in a position to recommend you to their company.

☐ ***Conventions and Trade Shows***

Probably the best source for spreading the word that you are looking for a new job. Even if you are unemployed, you must attend your trade or professional conventions.

☐ ***Consultants***

Consultants to your industry are important sources for job recommendations. They often are asked for names of people to recommend to their clients. Get to know the major consultants. When it is appropriate, provide them with leads for consulting assignments. They might feel that they owe you one.

☐ ***College Friends***

Keep in touch with the people that you went to college with, especially if you are working in the same city. You can also join and participate in alumni functions.

HOW TO BE THE RESULT OF A RECRUITMENT EFFORT (continued)

☐ *CPA Firms*

Accounting firms are excellent sources for financial people. Let them know that you would be interested in working for one of their clients.

☐ *Customers*

If you are in sales, let your customers know that you are looking for a new opportunity. If they have been impressed with your service, they could make recommendations to others. They are often called upon for referrals of top sales people.

☐ *Board of Director Members*

This is where top performance pays off. Because of your accomplishments, your name may reach the level of the board of directors. Because they often sit on several boards, board members, and especially venture capital representatives on the board, note major contributors for future assignments.

☐ *Employees of the Firm You Want to Join*

When you hear or read about a company that you would like to be a part of and you truly believe you could make a contribution, begin making a list of the names of the company's employees. Using the sources listed here, ask someone who works in the target company if they would make an introduction. You might refer to this as targeted networking.

☐ *Executive Search Firms*

Make it your business to establish a working relationship with several executive search recruiters. Make sure that they always have an updated resume as your career expands. You can establish a rapport with them by responding to their inquiry calls with recommendations of candidates. Use them to conduct searches for you and your company. Introduce them to others who might use their services. This is one of the most important sources for career advancement. Search firms often know about positions that never reach the public or industry.

☐ *Friends*

Let people in your social circle know that you are looking for a job. Be selective, as many people will not understand what you really do in your profession. Do not expect too much, and you will not lose a friend.

☐ *Instructors and Professors*

They are often contacted by companies for recommendations of current or past students. So keep in touch with department heads, particularly if you received an advanced degree. You can try to provide meaningful summer employment opportunities for professors or their students. They will appreciate the work opportunity, and you will establish some strong ties.

☐ *Job Fairs*

These are usually held in high technology cities. Although they are very impersonal, job fairs can lead to company interviews. Bring many copies of your resume for distribution. Only attend if you are unemployed, or if you do not care if word gets out that you are looking for a job.

☐ *Job Interviews*

Job interviews can turn out to be an excellent source for making contacts. Those that interview you may recognize your capabilities for a position different from the one for which you are being interviewed. Also, an interviewer may refer you to a friend or colleague at another company.

☐ *Outplacement Firms*

This is a source that can only be tapped by your employer, who pays the tab. Take advantage of their assistance. They are usually very professional and helpful.

☐ *Open Houses*

In areas of high employment or a shortage of some specific talent, companies may hold an open house for prospective employees and hiring managers to meet. This may be a good source if you are unemployed and fit into their demand category.

☐ *Reference Sources*

Serving as a reference to an employer or search firm for someone that they are considering may also help you. First, provide candid and honest responses to the questions. Then indicate to the caller that you have been looking at opportunities and would they be aware of any positions that might be suitable. At that point you will probably have a chance to describe your experience, or to send your resume.

☐ *Seminars*

Make it a point when attending a seminar or workshop to exchange business cards and establish contact with other attendees. Keep registration lists; a name from those business cards or registration lists may be the person to call when you are looking for a job change.

HOW TO BE THE RESULT OF A RECRUITMENT EFFORT (continued)

Career Counseling Firms

Career guidance and job change preparation and information can be very beneficial when you are in the job market. Most outplacement firms are excellent at this task. Unfortunately, they only accept counseling assignments from employers. As an individual, you cannot buy their services.

There are a number of firms that advertise career counseling or guidance services in the newspapers. They require you to pay a fee of from $1,000 to $2,000 and more to go through their program. Evaluate them very carefully to determine exactly what you are buying. Also try to get recommendations from people who have used their services.

Bookstores usually have many title selections in their career planning section. You will find information which covers much of the material that you will need to do your own job search.

Tips For Success

- Network every convention and trade show.
- Always have business cards with you. If you are unemployed, have a business card with your name, address, phone, message or fax number.
- Networking requires time and a proactive approach. Take a key contact to breakfast or lunch at least once a week.
- Submit an article for publication at least once every six to twelve months.
- Get to know the movers and shakers in your industry and community so that they recognize you by name.
- Serve as an officer or committee person for your industry or professional association, and do an exceptional job.

P A R T

2

The Resume Review Process: Getting Your 10 Seconds

RESUMES: A NECESSARY EVIL

Resumes can bring you in or do you in. They often are puff, and everyone knows it. They are more meaningful when solicited, rather than when they are received unsolicited. More criticism can be made about inclusions than exclusions. They may or may not differentiate you from the rest of the pack—which may be good or bad.

> Well-written resumes of mediocre people can result in more job opportunities than poorly written resumes of exceptional people.

Resumes can end up in the right or wrong hands, or they can be misinterpreted and end up in the wrong pigeonhole. No matter what, if your resume gets you an interview, then it is a piece of art!

What can make your resume a piece of art? When your resume compels the reader to want the real thing. You! The way you write and construct your resume and how you use it can make a real difference. The following looks at what happens to resumes received by companies and recruitment firms, and should give you a clue toward the look and content of your resume.

Ten Seconds May Be All You Get!

Human resources directors were asked, "When you receive an unsolicited resume, what happens?" The good news is that every resume is read. Maybe read is exaggerating the activity. Scan may be a more appropriate word—ten to fifty seconds tells the company recipient what to do with your resume.

In a small company, someone in the human resources department will often forward your resume to a specific hiring manager. The manager's speed in reviewing your resume will vary with the intensity of his or her current needs and the other pressures on him or her at that time. He or she may decide to phone you directly, or may pass your resume back to the human resources department with comments, such as retain your resume for the future.

A larger company may follow the same process. However, when a human resources person is assigned to a specific subgroup, your resume may float in that direction. At that point, a hiring manager may see your resume, or it may be kept in the human resources department.

RESUMES: A NECESSARY EVIL (continued)

The bottom line is that your resume may or may not be seen by the hiring manager when you send it *unsolicited* to the company human resources department. This should tell you two things about unsolicited resumes, and to whom you must become visible:

#1 An unsolicited resume sent to a human resources department typically *will not* generate a job opening.

#2 An unsolicited resume sent directly to a hiring manager, or even better, to a higher-up executive, could generate interest in creating a position for you.

A Solicited Resume Should Get Action, But...

Your resume falls into the solicited category when you send it to a company because of a phone request or a response to an advertisement. The former should definitely warrant attention and action, while the latter may be treated in batch form.

For example, you have received a phone call from either the hiring manager or someone within the human resources department. In both situations, you have had real dialogue with a named person. As a result of that conversation, you were invited to send a resume to the company. The significant thing is that you were asked to do so, and that you have a contact name.

Sending your resume in response to a request from the hiring manager will insure that your resume receives priority attention, as it was requested. On the other hand, sending your resume to the human resources person provides you with a name for future contact and follow-up. If your resume creates a positive impression on the human resources person, there is a high probability of having it forwarded to the hiring manager.

Sending a resume in response to an advertisement is like being asked to attend a dance with no guarantee that you will even be noticed. In areas where there is significant white-collar unemployment, and the required skills are stated generically, the ad response can be overwhelming. A single one-inch column advertisement for a chief financial officer, for example, produced over five hundred responses. Unless something in your resume package jumps out to attract attention, you will never get asked for an interview.

Although you are being solicited to submit a resume, responding to an ad is a marginal step over sending in an unsolicited resume. The ad typically asks you to send your resume to a department, not a specifically named person. The difference is that you know there is an opening for someone with your skills and experience. But again, it becomes a batch processing procedure. You may get thirty seconds, rather than the usual ten seconds.

Exercise: True or False

Answer the following statements:

	True	**False**
1. It is important to put as much information as possible in a resume.	☐	☐
2. Resumes get 10–50 seconds review in a typical organization.	☐	☐
3. An unsolicited resume sent to the human resources department is the most effective tactic for securing a job interview.	☐	☐
4. Companies usually respond quickly to resumes sent as the result of an advertisement.	☐	☐
5. Your resume may or may not be seen by the hiring manager if you send it to the human resources department.	☐	☐

Answers: 1. F **2.** T **3.** F **4.** F **5.** T

RESUMES: A NECESSARY EVIL (continued)

A Resume Received by an Employment Firm—How About Five Seconds!

There are two types of employment firms:

1. **Employment agencies,** and some recruitment firms whose business is to try to place you with a company. They typically receive a fee from the company only if they are successful in getting you employed. This is called a contingency recruitment firm.

2. **Search firms** and some recruitment firms whose business is to respond to a client's requests for specifically identified talent. A search firm's fee is not totally dependent on finding a person to fill a need; but their future existence is! A search firm's service is paid for by a combination of a retainer and/or progress fees from the client. The minimum salary level that a search firm recruits for is usually $75,000.

The term recruitment firm spans both categories, and defies a clear definition. Although a contingency recruitment firm may handle executive-level positions, a retained search firm works only on the more significant recruitment engagements. The contingency type is a placement firm, and the retained type is a search firm.

A resume sent to a placement firm will receive sufficient attention to determine:

- If your experience is in line with the type of companies in which they have established some rapport

- Who in the placement firm should make the contact either by calling or sending your resume to a company

You should receive attention from a placement firm which handles your classification of experience. Some may just handle software engineers. Others may have made their mark in placing accounting and financial personnel. Placement firms earn their income by placing people within their specialty. Therefore, it is important to determine which firms have a specialty in your field.

With placement firms, your resume may often be the main tool with which they conduct business. Most will at least phone you, and some will even interview you in person. If the placement firm is industry specialized, they may duplicate your resume and send it unsolicited to companies within your industry. If they are functionally oriented, such as accounting or data processing, they may send your resume to local employers.

Placement firms may send your resume in direct response to a job order that they have received from a company. In those instances, a qualified candidate, or resume, is solicited. The rapport between the placement agency and the company may be very valuable in insuring that your resume receives attention. In times of high unemployment, or where your skills are shared by many, a company is less likely to pay a placement agency's fees, and is more inclined to advertise.

A retained search firm, because it responds only to a client's request, takes a different approach with your resume. Your unsolicited resume represents a possible future candidate for one of their clients (the chance of receiving your resume at the time that they are searching for someone with your experience is extremely slim). Your resume also is a source of candidates for them. Because of this, your resume will probably receive a very quick review.

At first glance your resume will indicate whether you have the type of experience which they are typically retained to find. If you are a banker, and they have not had a banking client in ten years, more than likely your resume will be passed over. On the other hand, if you are a sales executive in the game or toy industry and they have many consumer products clients, your resume will be a keeper.

This means that your resume will be read, coded and become a part of their data bank of prospects and sources. Who codes your resume and how it is coded will play an important and vital role in your future. Finding you again depends on their retrieval system, and how you were entered.

Directories such as *The Directory of Executive Recruiters,* from the Consultants Bookstore, Templeton Road, Fitzwilliam, NH 03447, (603) 585-2200, are a must if you are sending unsolicited resumes to recruitment firms. The directory will tell you the name, address, and key contact within each recruitment firm. It also identifies the recruitment firm's functional and industry specialty. Without this information you may be wasting correspondence on firms that may give you less than five seconds.

WHAT'S IN A NAME?

In a word, everything!

> Never send a resume to a department, company or search firm without addressing it to a particular person by name, not just title.

Do not assume that a name in a directory is the correct name for a specific title. Titles and responsibilities are dynamic; directories are static.

An unsolicited resume should be sent to the person who is two positions above the point where you think you should enter the company.

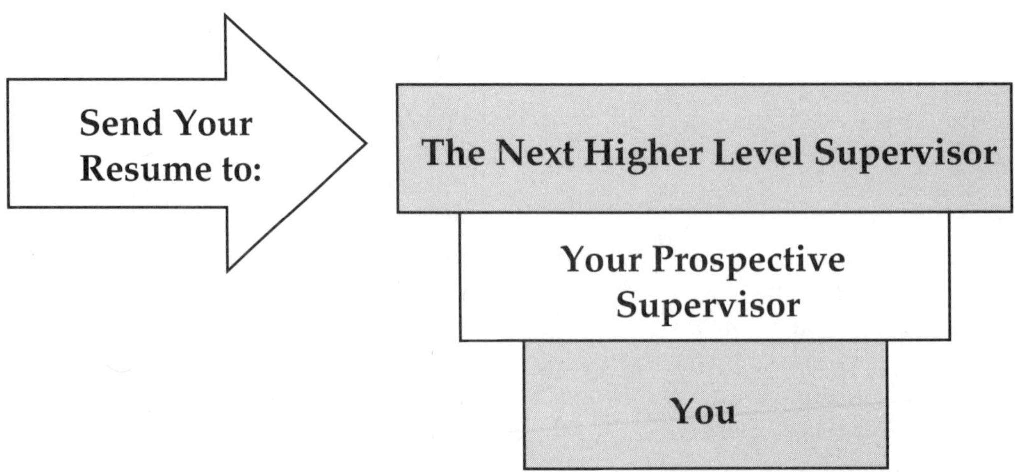

If you are seeking a regional sales manager position, and that position reports to a national sales manager, then you should send your resume to the next person in the chain of command, the vice president of sales. Why? Because organizational changes, strategic planning, and budget commitments, all those things that affect personnel changes and hires, flow downward.

The purpose of sending an unsolicited resume to a company is to create a need for you and a desire to meet you. The person who can create a new position or influence a hiring decision is typically above the position to which you would report. The direct hiring manager, the person to whom you would report, may have a budgeted opening for someone like you, and could well make the decision. But if their supervisor was stimulated by your resume, the word would come down from above.

Case Study: GO TO THE TOP

A military officer just about to leave the service sent an excellent cover letter and resume to the president of a company. The president, in turn, passed it on to the human resources director, suggesting that the officer be brought in for interviews with their manufacturing department. The human resources director would never have considered this person for a position in manufacturing, because the officer did not meet the usual criteria. (This story quickly points out the best place to send your unsolicited resume.)

Follow the same rule if you are responding to an employment advertisement: send your resume to a specifically named person two levels above your entry position. This may take some homework, but it will give you an edge.

There are several ways to find out the name of the person to whom you should send your resume.

1. You can call the company directly and ask the operator for the name of the person who holds the title or position that you want to address. If you are not certain what that title or position is, always go for a higher level rather than a lower level person who might not have hiring decision-making responsibilities. If the operator cannot help you, he or she will usually forward your call to the human resources department.

   Whomever you speak to, you should say: "I would like to send some correspondence to the vice president of sales (or the manufacturer manager), and would like his or her name." Do not indicate that you are responding to an advertisement or that you are sending in a resume. In most cases, you will get the name immediately.

2. Industry buying directories, professional trade association directories, and other scores of reference books are available at most libraries, and can be very useful. However, be sure the directory or source which you are using was published or updated within the last six months. You should also phone the companies to verify the names.

3. Use your networking skills to locate someone who works, or knows someone who works in the target organization. Not only will this method provide the right name, but you may also learn more about the person to whom you are directing your resume, the hiring manager and the company. The more you know, the better you will be able to personalize your cover letter.

Exercise: Gathering Information

Now that you know the benefits of "aiming high," it's your turn to go to the top. For a company you are interested in working for, answer the following:

1. I am interested in working for (company name)_____.
2. The title for my position would probably be ____________________.
3. The person I would report to is ____________________, and his or her title is ____________________.
4. This person's supervisor is (name and title)_____.
5. If this is not a company officer, what is the first officer's title to whom the person identified in #4 reports?

   Name: ____________________ Title: ____________________

Responding to ''Blind Ads''

Companies run blind employment ads to keep their recruitment confidential, or to eliminate the task of responding to all of the people who reply to the ad. Without debating the value of blind ads, how should you respond when you have no company or name identification?

The blind ad may provide sufficient clues as to the company's industry, size, location, products or other identifying information that you can use to narrow your choice of prospects. Using your network and a few well-placed calls, you may be able to reduce the choices to a few. Then follow the guidelines to identify and select the correct name to address your cover letter and resumes to. You may end up sending your packet to several different companies.

Suppose your identification efforts are not successful. If the ad is irresistible, then you should address it to the title of the person two levels above the position. Do not refer to the ad, but be sure that your cover letter emphasizes your strengths as related to the ad.

In some instances, you may need to protect you own identity if you suspect that the ad could be your current employer. Have a friend (or fake a friend) send a cover letter describing your capabilities, indicating that there is some concern about revealing your name until you know who ran the ad. If they respond, you will have the advantage of knowing their identity.

Tips for Success

- Never send a resume to a human resources department, unless you are applying for a human resources position.
- Always send your resume to a specifically named person, not just a title.
- Always send your unsolicited resumes or responses to advertisements to the person who is two levels above your entry level.

P A R T

3

Your Resume: An Interview Makes It a Piece of Art

TWO BASIC RESUME STYLES

There are two basic styles of resumes, and, of course, several unique hybrids. You should stick to one of the two basic styles: chronological or functional.

Style #1: Chronological Resumes

A chronological resume describes your experiences and accomplishments in a reverse chronological order, beginning with your current or most recent position. Positions are presented under a heading that includes your position and the company name. Specific accomplishments are described under each employer heading. The vast majority of resumes are presented in a chronological style.

Chronological resumes present your qualifications in an easy to follow manner, tracing your progression from job to job. The reader can note what you accomplished for each company, and determine if your history is appropriate for their current or future interests. Because of its ease of interpretation, the chronological resume is preferred by most companies and recruitment firms.

An example of a chronological resume is shown on pages 24 and 25.

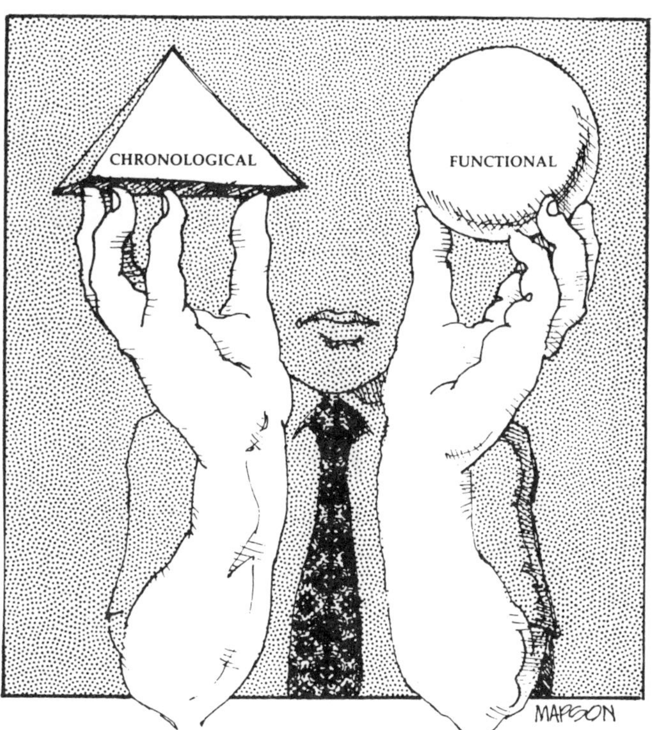

James C. Garland, CPA
3427 Bakers Road
Northbrook, Illinois 60036
Business (312) 555-4687 Residence (708) 555-9831

PROFESSIONAL SUMMARY

Seasoned financial executive with a strong operational background in retail and manufacturing environment. Four years of ''big six'' public accounting experience with extensive systems knowledge and analytical skills. Skilled in planning and implementing organizational change.

EXPERIENCE

Specialty Crafts, Inc., Northbrook, Illinois 1991 to Present

Leading specialty retailer generating $500 million in sales with 650 craft stores nationally and two 500,000-square-foot distribution centers.

Vice President and Controller
Responsible for SEC reporting, general accounting, merchandise control, budgeting and operating analysis, as well as strategic planning.

- Developed comprehensive valuation of store and distribution center inventory, which led to the reduction of interim inventory levels by over $15 million.
- Originated SEC reporting including all 10-Qs and the 10K. Coordinated the external auditors' year-end work.
- Prepared the annual report, which included the restatement of prior periods for divestiture and extraordinary items.
- Identified organizational inefficiencies and implemented a new structure which saved the company $500,000 in real administrative costs annually.

Tools 'R Us, Inc., Chicago, Illinois 1980 to 1991

$1 billion marketing and distribution company.

Controller (1987 to 1991)
Reported to the president and sat on the Executive Committee. Responsible for managing financial functions to meet the strategic needs of the business, including cash management and credit, MIS, accounting, merchandise control, financial planning, budgeting, and operational analysis.

- Converted the internal inventory valuation system from weighted average cost to standard cost, producing a 12–15% increase in inventory turns, and allowing a much more detailed inventory shrinkage analysis.

Tools 'R Us, Inc. (continued)

- Reduced bad debt by 40% to a level of industry leadership through tightened credit procedures and constant evaluation of the organization.
- Developed a method of analyzing risk/profitability ratios for major customers which influenced subsequent pricing policies.
- Negotiated a 20% reduction in retail bank credit card fees.

Accounting Director (1984 to 1987)
Responsible for all internal management reporting, corporate reporting, full trial balance, accounting and control, payroll, computer operations, and branch accounting for over 3,000 cost and profit centers.

Financial Planning and Analysis Director (1980 to 1984)
Recruited to set up a new position for formalizing the planning and budgeting process.

Bingham Machinery Corp., Gary, Indiana 1978 to 1980

Prime manufacturer of heavy machinery used in earth moving and construction.

Controller's Staff Analyst
Responsible for analyzing the $750 million operation and providing the technical accounting process and procedures to produce a common financial reporting system. Originally joined the company as an *Auditor.*

Ernst & Anderson, Chicago, Illinois 1972 to 1978

Senior Accountant on the Audit Staff
Supported a variety of clients ranging from Fortune 1000 companies to small privately held firms. Also performed tax and write-up work.

EDUCATION

MBA, Northwestern University, 1980
BBA, Accounting, University of Illinois, 1972

PROFESSIONAL

Certified Public Accountant
Member of AICPA and the Illinois Society of CPAs

TWO BASIC RESUME STYLES (continued)

Using the "reverse" chronological resume of James Garland as a guide, list below your work history for the past ten years. Only include the company name, your job titles and the dates for each position held.

1. ______________________
____
____

2. ______________________
____
____

3. ______________________
____
____

4. ______________________
____
____

5. ______________________
____
____

6. ______________________
____
____

Style #2: Functional Resume

A functional resume, on the other hand, describes your strengths and accomplishments according to particular areas of experience. For example, if you are a vice president of finance, you might relate your experiences under such categories as treasury and banking relationships, cost controls, reporting systems, and financial management. At the end of the resume, employers and positions are listed in a reverse chronological fashion. The reader must, therefore, guess which function was carried out at which company.

A functional resume is appropriate when:

- Your chronological history would not show a progressive increase in responsibility.
- You want to change or reduce the impact of your current industry, and thus want to demonstrate your functional strength and experience.
- You have changed jobs too often, and want the dates to appear at the end of the resume, rather than showing up as each position is described.

An example of a functional resume is shown on pages 27 and 28.

CYNTHIA L. MORGAN
1730 West Mesa Road • San Francisco, California 95455 • (415) 555-7986

PROFESSIONAL SUMMARY

Extensive management background in sales, marketing and communications. Track record in new product introductions and national roll-outs. Responsible for significant market share gains for established products.

ACCOMPLISHMENTS

Management

- Managed manufacturers' representative organization consisting of twenty-two manufacturers' lines covering thirteen Midwestern states with a staff of one hundred sixty. Doubled the business to $24 million within two years.
- Directed and managed the creative development team for the successful introduction of "Natural Skin," making it the #1 consumer brand name for its classification.
- Co-founded a marketing consulting firm generating over $8 million in consulting revenue by the third year. Established the firm as one of the leading innovators in consumer brands' marketing.
- Recruited, trained and managed a national sales organization that produced $32 million in revenue in eighteen months for a new line of lip gloss.

Sales & Marketing

- Led territorial sales region three years in a row. Was the first woman to receive the highest President's Award.
- Identified a new market for an existing product, tripling revenues to over $60 million in five years. Awarded the "Rookie Marketing Contributor-of-the-Year".
- Managed all North American sales for an HBA manufacturer, increasing sales from $18 million to $26 million in one year.
- Established first Western states sales territory, building revenues from zero to $5.5 million in two years.

CYNTHIA L. MORGAN **Page 2**

Communications

- Created product name, package design, advertising, trade show booth and new corporate identity for a line of specialty skin creams.

- Reversed long-term share decline of Spoofs' Shaving Cream with an award-winning ad campaign.

EMPLOYMENT HISTORY

Morgan & Stellman, Inc., San Francisco, California 1990 to present
Vice President and Co-Founder
Consumer goods marketing consulting firm.

The Caldberry Company, Chicago, Illinois 1988 to 1990
Vice President, Sales and Marketing
Major food and HBA brokerage firm.

Adrian Klien, Inc., New York, New York 1985 to 1988
Marketing Manager, "Natural Skin" Brand
International cosmetics corporation.

The Everette Group, Trenton, New Jersey 1980 to 1985
National Sales Manager
Specialty cosmetic products company.

The Buckanell Corporation, New York, New York 1972 to 1980
Product Sales Manager
Consumer products division of this Fortune 100 firm.

O'Brien Advertising, Chicago, Illinois 1970 to 1972
Senior Account Manager
Midwest consumer products advertising agency.

EDUCATION

BBA, Marketing, University of Iowa, 1970

MBA, Marketing, City College of New York, 1976

Exercise: Job Function Identification

Using the functional resume of Cynthia Morgan as a guide, identify three (3) functions (i.e. General Management, Sales, Finance, etc.) you consider are your major strengths. These should be functions that you can convince a prospective employer are areas in which you can make a significant contribution. Under each of these three functions, list the employers and job titles held where accomplishments could be expanded upon to emphasize your contribution toward these three functions. One employer may serve several functions.

1. ______________________________

____

____

2. ______________________________

____

____

3. ______________________________

____

____

Whichever resume style you use, it is important to remember that your visibility to the reader will depend on what you say and how it is presented. You may make it easier for the reader to follow your resume, but lose out on the opportunity to have an interview. Or your resume may be difficult to follow, but sufficiently enticing to make the reader want to meet you in person. The net result is that your resume is a sales tool. As such, it has to stimulate the action you desire—to get an interview. Therefore, what must your resume contain?

TWO BASIC RESUME STYLES (continued)

Every Resume, No Matter What...

Every resume, no matter what the style, must include certain basic information. You need to identify where and when you worked, the position(s) that you held, your accomplishments and your education.

Company Identification

A description of each company that you worked for should include the company name, city, state, and a one-line sentence that describes the company. That one-line sentence is important to the reader.

The Fortune 500 companies, or perhaps even the Fortune 1000, are almost household names. But with recent mergers and acquisitions, the reader may not know that New Bicycle Concepts, Inc. is a part of Horseless Carriages, Ltd. This is also true of companies which have a strong local following, but may be unheard of five hundred miles away.

Readers like to relate to a company. The description usually will tell the reader the industry in which you worked, and, perhaps, the size of the company and its reputation. If the one-liner is missing, the reader has the option to phone you to find out this information—a plus. Or they may decide when giving you your five seconds that the extra effort to find out this information is not worth the time.

If the company name has strength, and/or the industry is important to your career progression, then by all means, include the one-liner. If neither of the above are important, then you have a choice of whether to include this information, although you probably should include it. It shouldn't hurt your chances, and it does help someone to code you for a future retrieval.

Dates

An interviewer will probe your resume for the exact months of employment with each of your employers. This is to determine if there are any unaccountable time gaps. However, it is only necessary to state the date in "years" to define tenure on your resume.

Those who have had several (hopefully not many) short-term positions during their career use "years" to omit jobs of less than one year. This can be dangerous, and jeopardize a good opportunity if and when your real job history is discovered. You must operate on the premise that discrepancies on your resume will be uncovered. Those that get caught often end up in a worse position.

Position/Title

When identifying the position(s) you held within a company, always use your last title. This is usually the highest level position that you held with the company, and the one that you wish bestowed on you. If you had more then one significant position or title within the same company, then identify these separately.

Your most recent or current position is extremely important. A company or recruitment firm usually codes your resume based on your last or current position. You may have had a successful career in sales, and are now in a top sales management or sales executive role. Your cover letter states that you are now looking for a general management position. Guess where you will most likely be categorized? You're right if you said sales management. So the last title you use is very important.

Exercise: Employer Identification

In the space below, develop a complete employer identification for each employer listed on page 26, including the company name, dates and position identification for your current or most recent position. Be sure to include the company one-liner.

____

____

____

____

____

____

TWO BASIC RESUME STYLES (continued)

Accomplishments

A company usually seeks a candidate who has a track record in making bottom-line contributions. Accomplishments separate the winners from the losers. It is vital that your accomplishments jump off the page.

Accomplishments strongly influence your opportunities for personal interviews. They must compel readers to want to see you!

A man who had spent the last few years in the executive search business decided to return to industry. He had received and reviewed hundreds of resumes, and knew what they should contain. Prior to his search career, he had held very responsible positions, and was well known in several industries. His resume contained many significant accomplishments, however, they were buried in paragraphs. They just didn't jump off the page.

After he ''bulletized'' his accomplishments, and strengthened them with numbers (dollar figures or percentages) to show maximum contribution to the bottom-line, his resume was dramatically improved. Even though he was ''in the industry,'' and knew what a good resume should include, some points just slipped by. He made a few changes in his resume and the important points now jumped out at the reader.

One approach to identifying your accomplishments is to make a list of the results you achieved during the past ten years. For each year, try to come up with a minimum of at least two results. In every possible example, quantify the results, relating it to the bottom-line. Start each accomplishment with an action verb. Here are some examples:

- Developed a patent program, resulting in six new patents filed during the first year, establishing a proprietary advantage for the company.

- Developed a business plan for a start-up company, generating venture capital financing of $8 million.

- Recruited top engineering and management talent, achieving an 85% acceptance rate on offers made.

- Implemented manufacturing control systems (MRP and JIT) and production automation programs, achieving industry-wide lowest cost manufacturing position.
- Achieved 400% sales increase in eighteen months by redirecting and energizing the sales program.
- Established a foreign sales corporation, saving company $500 thousand annually in tax benefits on export sales.
- Doubled sales in six months while improving gross margins to over 50%.
- In two years took the division from 7% to 12% net profit via new product introduction.
- Increased cash position from $11 million to $28 million in one year.
- Expanded previously undeveloped territory, and increased revenue from $80 thousand to over $1 million.

Exercise: Accomplishment Identification

On a separate piece of paper, develop a list of at least 10 accomplishments that cover the past five years, using the above examples as a guide.

Education

Does a company really check the educational credentials that you state on your resume? Recent informal surveys indicate that companies are now spending additional time checking references, including your education. Therefore, as in any part of your resume, DO NOT LIE! Whatever you state in writing must be verifiable, or you could get caught and miss a major opportunity.

Case Study: THE NONEXISTENT DEGREE

Susan was an extremely qualified chief financial officer candidate for a West Coast think tank. Preliminary phone discussions with the human resources manager were very positive. She learned that the majority of the employees held masters or doctorate degrees. Personal interviews with company staff, including the president, confirmed that Susan and the company would be right for one another.

But the human resources manager did her due diligence, and Susan's college degree could not be verified. When approached, Susan stuck to her story, saying that perhaps the records were under her maiden name. Still the records could not be found. Susan continued her stand, saying that maybe the college had lost her records. This process of checking and denial continued for about a week.

The human resources manager finally told Susan that without this verification no offer would be forthcoming. Two days later, Susan phoned to say that she had not received the degree, and that hearing that all the executives at the think tank were well educated, she had thought that she would never get the job without a degree. She had thought wrong.

Susan made a big blunder. How could a company hire a chief financial officer who had lied on her resume, and then had continued to lie when confronted? A position with high-level financial responsibility had to be held by a person whom they could trust.

How should you state your degrees? Include the degree received, the school, location, and the year bestowed. The year you received your degree will provide the reader with your approximate age. If you believe that your age could be a drawback (an unlawful discrimination act) in obtaining an interview (the sole purpose of the resume), then leave it out.

Example:

Masters of Business Administration, University of California, Berkeley, California, 1985

Suppose that you did not receive a particular degree, but still wanted to provide information about your education.

The only dates you should use when you do not have a degree are the dates that you attended. A single year may be misleading and give the reader the impression that you did receive the degree.

> Masters of Business Administration Program, University of California, Berkeley, California, 1983–1985.

What if you feel your education over-qualifies you for the position, and you are embarrassed by your doctorate in economics when applying for a sales position. By not listing the degree, you would, perhaps, leave an unexplained period of time, which may cause more questions than the degree. List the degree! The advanced degree may arouse curiosity, such as "Why would a doctorate in economics want this job? I want to meet this person and find out."

Exercise: Organize Your Educational Background

List your degrees/credentials, using the previous resumes as guides. For each institution, include the degree awarded, your major, the institution, and the year granted or years attended if a degree was not granted.

1. ______________________________

____

____

2. ______________________________

____

____

3. ______________________________

____

____

TWO BASIC RESUME STYLES (continued)

Tips for Success

- Select the resume style that best sells your capabilities. Choose the one that emphasizes your strengths and plays down your shortcomings.
- Create accomplishments that are compelling and indicate strong bottom-line contributions.
- Develop accomplishments for the most recent ten to fifteen years. Then select the best to show a broad scope of experience which highlights your strengths.
- For positions beyond fifteen years, state the name of your employer and your position. List them only if they contribute to, or build up to, your most recent position.
- Have a draft of your resume reviewed by someone in the recruitment business.

RESUME OPTIONS: ENHANCEMENTS OR DETRACTORS?

Options should be included only when they will enhance the image that you want to create. You must feel that the reader will perceive the options that you use as positive traits, experiences, or circumstances which back up your qualifications for the position which you are seeking. Although you do not have to include any options, here are a few examples:

Position Objective

A Position Objective is a short statement that tells the reader the title of the position for which you are applying. Human Resources Director/Manager, District Sales Manager, Loan Officer, or Materials Manager are just a few examples.

Putting an objective on your resume is optional. It can sometimes do you more harm than good. It tends to pigeonhole you to a specific title or category. Remember the 5 second review. If your objective says or implies the wrong title or position, you may be missed or misplaced.

The objective is usually stated at the top of the resume. It can thus limit your options right from the start. Suppose you had an objective that stated ''General Management or Chief Operating Officer.'' You have had a solid sales and marketing career, and now want to move into general management. However, the company has a plum position for a vice president of sales. Unfortunately, whoever coded you placed your resume in the wrong pile. You may never even be considered for this excellent opportunity.

You may argue that the opposite could also happen—you could be coded as a sales executive, and miss out on an opportunity for a general management position. Perhaps, but a company or recruiter looking for a general manager candidate with a sales background would also look at candidates who have held executive sales positions.

RESUME OPTIONS: ENHANCEMENTS OR DETRACTORS? (continued)

Summary Statement

Instead of stating an objective, some people use a summary statement, such as:

> *An engineering executive with over fifteen years experience directing the development of state-of-the-art winglenuts. Patents have secured a company proprietary position resulting in world leadership of winglenuts and related products.*

The use of a summary statement is softer than an objective, in that it leads up to what you may be qualified for, rather than blatantly stating what you want. Although it is acceptable on a resume, this statement would be better placed in your cover letter. You can then modify it to suit the position for which it is intended.

Interests

The use of interests should convey an image of you. ''Enjoy jogging, tennis and hiking,'' would imply that you are in good physical shape. It is, therefore, a positive statement.

Affiliations

''American Production and Inventory Control Society'' or listing any other professional association *might* indicate your interest in continued personal improvement in professional skills. However, listing too many (more than three) may indicate that you are a ''joiner,'' and may take too much time away from business.

Personal Data

"Thirty-seven years old; one wife; one child." This is an actual quote from a resume. Perhaps the author though that it brought a sense of humor to a rather dull history. Forget it!

"Married, two children." This could indicate stability; but not necessarily. Leave this information for the interview.

"Excellent health." Nobody ever puts down "Poor health." Forget either one.

References

"Excellent references are available." They will be required at some stage, but do not include that statement on the resume.

Papers, Patents or Articles

If papers, patents or articles substantially add to your credibility, then by all means include one or two titles as a sample. Do not provide a complete list on your resume. Instead, have an addendum available at the interview in which you list the appropriate material. There is one exception however.

When you are applying for a research or technical position, or a "publish or perish" position, and have written papers or applied for patents which may demonstrate your advanced technological capabilities, then include this addendum when submitting your resume. However, for all the rest who have written papers, the following should be sufficient:

"Publications: Author of *Levitation For All,* Wild Stuff Press, 1993. Numerous articles on "Gravity, Is It Real?" in selected scientific journals."

MISCELLANEOUS MECHANICS AND LEFTOVERS

- **Printing:** Use laser printing or off-set printing only; NEVER use dot matrix printing.
- **Stapling:** Always staple the pages of your resume together. Never staple your cover letter to your resume.
- **Pictures:** Do not send one!
- **Business Cards:** Do not send one!
- **Binders:** Do not use *any* type of binder for your resume.
- **Paper:** 8½″ × 11″. Always use white or off-white.
- **Highlighting:** Do not use a highlighter marker to emphasize points on your resume.
- **Pages:** Resumes should be either one or two pages. Never type on the back of a page.
- **Response Forms:** Do not enclose a postcard or a fax form for the reader to respond to your resume.
- **Contact Information:** Make sure that you have your name, address, and phone number on your resume. Also have your name on the top of the second page.
- **Paper Clips:** Can be used to attach your cover letter to your resume.
- **Envelopes:** Standard size for folded or flat mailing.
- **Resumes-for-Two:** Never include more than one resume per person per envelope.
- **Return Address Stickers:** Do not use them!

Tips for Success

- Don't use overkill on your resume. More information is not necessarily better. Try to provide a reason, even just for curiosity, for the reader to invite you for a personal interview.
- Use options *only* when they will significantly add to your capabilities or image.
- Save personal information for the interview.
- If you can not confine your resume to two pages, get professional help.
- Pay attention to details. This may be the one and only opportunity for you to get a job offer.
- Keep your style conservative throughout the resume.
- If you are requested to fax your resume, always follow up with your hard copy.

P A R T

4

Your Cover Letter: It's a Wrap and a Must!

COVER LETTERS: WHAT EVERY RESUME MUST HAVE

A cover letter is a marketing tool that *must* accompany every resume you mail to a prospective employer. It:

- Introduces you, and it establishes rapport between you and the reader.
- Personalizes your resume by addressing it to a specific person.
- Enhances your resume by emphasizing some significant items.
- Allows you to summarize or state your job objective, tailored to the specific company or position.

Case Study: GETTING TOO CREATIVE

Imagine a cover letter sent on green letterhead. The writer told of his virtues as a successful sales executive who could produce a lot of "green" for his next employer. He concluded his letter with a signature, *$teve $mith*. This letter just could not be ignored.

Rather than being tossed in the circular file, the recruiter who had received the letter phoned Steve. The recruiter felt compelled to comment on his unprofessional letter style, signature and accompanying green resume. In response, Steve said, "It got your attention."

The recruiter agreed, but indicated that Steve got his attention for the wrong reason. Although Steve had a pretty decent track record—achieving some significant sales results—his approach gave the impression of lacking professional taste and style. The recruiter told Steve that he was concerned about recommending Steve to one of his clients.

Two weeks later a more professionally written letter and resume were received from Steve. Along with the package came a note of thanks.

This story illustrates that a cover letter definitely has an impact on its readers. It sets the tone for the resume that follows. A reader who is turned-off by your cover letter may never even look at your resume. Therefore, be sure the image which you portray in your letter represents the image that you want to leave with the reader.

THE IMPORTANT BASICS

Here are eight rules for constructing a cover letter that will give you an edge:

#1. **Get to the point of your letter in the first paragraph.** The first sentence must have some punch. Tell the reader why you are writing. Do not use a lot of "fluff," and don't be cute. You should not tell the reader how wonderful they are, or how great the company is. And do not tell the reader that someone influential suggested that you write, unless you are *absolutely* positive that the reader will know your reference.

#2. **The first paragraph should stimulate the reader to want to meet you.** Provide one of your strongest accomplishments—one that will quickly be perceived as a very strong benefit to the reader. Or, if you *really* have a connection to the reader or company, use it.

#3. **The second paragraph should add one or two more accomplishments that are indicative of your overall strengths.** Quantify these accomplishments, and show how they affected the bottom-line of your current or previous employer(s). This should reinforce the reader's desire to meet you.

If you are responding because of an advertisement, tie your accomplishments to the requirements in the ad, but *do not refer to the ad in your letter.*

#4. **The final or last paragraph should provide a sound close, and the action that you will take.** If you say that you will call within a few weeks, be sure that you do it. (Do not tell recruitment firms that you will call them. You can be sure that they will phone you if there is a reason.)

#5. **Do not state your compensation level or your salary requirements in the letter.** You may immediately eliminate yourself for consideration as your compensation may be either too low or too high. Always sell yourself first; then compensation will take its normal course. (There is more information on compensation later.)

#6. **If your cover letter extends to the bottom of the first page, it's too long.** Readers do not have or will not take the time to read too much about you. Keep your cover letter short and strong.

#7. **Always, without exception, address a cover letter to a specific person.** (Remember, send your resume two levels above your entry position.)

#8. **Do not say what you want *from* the company, but indicate what you can *contribute* to the company.** Minimize the use of "I" and "me," and use "you" and "your."

Some Additional Tips

- "You may contact me at the above address or telephone number." *Don't waste this line!*

- "The last decade of American business has witnessed considerable restructuring and targeting and economic disruption. I have managed successfully in this environment and am well prepared to continue to do the same." *Who cares? This and 50¢ may get you a cup of coffee, but not an interview.*

- "I am writing to you because of your firm's excellent reputation and expertise in financial searches." *It's nice to hear that their reputation for the few financial searches that they have conducted has spread so far. However, they neither have a reputation nor expertise in financial searches. This person didn't do their homework.*

- "Your name was given to me by ____________________, a former client of yours." *They never heard of ____________________; and would never forget the name of a client!*

- Here are some examples, taken from real cover letters, of what *not to say.*

  "My compensation package prior to leaving included:

  Salary: $84,000
  Bonus: $21,000

  The minimum compensation I would consider is $70,000." *Never mention compensation. Acceptance of a 70% reduction in pay indicates desperation or lack of self-confidence.*

Exercise: Write Your First Paragragh

Review rules 1 and 2 on page 46. Write a powerful first paragraph for your cover letter. Make it irresistible and compelling for an employer to invite you in for an interview.

AN EXAMPLE OF A GOOD COVER LETTER STYLE

Addressed to specific name and title.

June 2, 19XX

Mr. Morgan R. Haines
President
Haines Executive Search Recruiters
1213 Post Street
Valley View, California 90107

Dear Mr. Haines:

He claims to be a generalist; not a specific functional person such as a sales manager or controller. Only one "my," with emphasis on what he can do for clients.

Sales, marketing, manufacturing operations, asset management, employee relations and finance have been my areas of concentration and expertise. Are you aware of a company who could profit by an experienced general manager who has had significant P & L responsibility?

Highlights of my accomplishments in the consumer products industry include:

Numbers stated in accomplishments are always impressive, but obviously would need to be verified. The point is, this person appears to have some significant achievements. You are almost compelled to read the resume to find out who the companies were, and if his success could contribute to one of his clients.

- Turning around a deeply troubled company, improving return on equity from 4% to 31%, return on sales from 0.8% to more than 14%, and return on assets from 2% to 30%, generating a 14-fold increase in profitability.
- Growing the core business to $100 million from $54 million, while improving margins 50% and achieving 95% complete and on-time shipments. Making up loss of $25 million in revenues when three unprofitable divisions were sold.
- While becoming the dominant market leader in markets served, grew orders 18% and revenues 15% compounded annually for each of the last five years.

A nice and safe closing statement. No promises of action, such as "I will call you next week." Displays self-confidence and knowledge of how to work with search firms, or for that matter, other executives. He knows that if he has stimulated interest, he will be called.

I would appreciate the opportunity to personally present my credentials to you, and explore how I might contribute to one of your client organization's growth and profitability.

Thank you for your consideration. I look forward to hearing from you soon.

Sincerely,

THE IMPORTANT BASICS (continued)

Sample Opening Lines

Below are some opening lines for good cover letters. These are variations of actual letters received.

Opening Line #1

"Do you know of a company in need of an executive with seventeen years of progressive Operations Management experience? A client of yours could capitalize on my proven ability to enhance manufacturing efficiency, quality, and profitability."

Opening Line #2

*"Please don't let the word "**President**" on the enclosed resume limit your perspective of my skill set. At this stage of life, job satisfaction means more to me than titles. If one of your clients needs an executive who can build business strategically, either from the ground up or by redirecting focus, then we should talk."*

Opening Line #3

"A program I completed for one of my employers generated more than $1 million annually in savings. My management and engineering accomplishments have demonstrated a successful record of increasing productivity, reducing costs, and improving operations in a variety of business environments. Perhaps one of your clients could profit by similar results."

Opening Line #4

"After my two-year assignment as President, the company was successfully rebuilt for the purpose of enhancing its divestiture value. If a diverse, proven track record of business building and turnarounds for major consumer packaged goods companies equates with the needs of one of your clients, please let me know."

Tips for Success

- Never handwrite a cover letter! Always use laser-quality printing.
- Use 20#, white or off-white, 8½″ by 11″ bond paper.
- Place the cover letter in front of the resume in the envelope.
- Be sure that you sign the letter.
- Be sure to check for spelling and grammar mistakes.
- Avoid using graphics or printed pictures on letters.
- Make sure that your name, contact information and the date are on the letter.
- Be sure that the letter is addressed to the same person whose name appears on the envelope. (Commercial mailers sometimes put the wrong letter in the envelope.)
- Don't forget to enclose the resume!

P A R T

5

Interviewing: Preparing for the Test

PREPARING FOR THE INTERVIEW

The ultimate test as to whether you are in the Right Place at the Right Time with the Right Credentials is the face-to-face interview.

An employer has two interview objectives:

1. To determine if you are qualified to fill a current open position requirement.

2. To determine if you are qualified to be considered for future positions.

You have only one objective: TO GET A JOB OFFER!

Exercise: Are You Really *Ready?*

Answer the following questions to test your knowledge of preparing for an interview:

	TRUE	FALSE
1. If your interview is scheduled on ''casual'' Friday, you should dress casually to fit in.	☐	☐
2. You should know your resume thoroughly, and remember which years you worked for each employer.	☐	☐
3. College degrees prior to fifteen years ago can not be verified by an employer.	☐	☐
4. Do not get to the interview early, as you may appear too anxious.	☐	☐
5. The only important interview is with the hiring manager.	☐	☐
6. Finalist candidates may have five or more company interviews.	☐	☐
7. You should be prepared to cite many quantitative examples of your accomplishments.	☐	☐
8. You can not obtain information about a privately held company prior to the interview.	☐	☐
9. The smell from smoking can be a turn-off to the interviewer.	☐	☐
10. You should treat the hiring manager's staff respectfully, as they can affect a hiring decision.	☐	☐

An interview is a sales presentation. The more you know about the buyer (the prospective employer) and the product (yourself), the better the chance you have for making the sale (receiving an offer and landing the job). What should you know before going on an interview?

Answers: True: 2, 6, 7, 9, 10. False: 1, 3, 5, 8

THE PROSPECTIVE EMPLOYER

You should get to know the employer before you arrive for your interview. Information is available through the public library, newspaper libraries, trade journals, the Chamber of Commerce, stock brokerage firms, bankers, and friends and colleagues. Use your network to find out all you can about the company.

Interview Preparation Quick-Check

In order to be prepared for an interview, find out the following information about a company you are interested in and fill in the blanks:

1. The position for which you are applying: ______________________

____

2. The department and the manager to whom you would report: __________

____

3. Basic company data, such as the number of employees, products or services, number of years in business, and revenues: ______________

____

____

4. The style and personality of the managers and company: ____________

____

____

5. The company's customers. Who are they? ____________________

____

____

6. The company's reputation among its employees, customers and the financial community: ______________________________

____

____

Exercise: Making A Positive Impact

There are several things that you must do or know in preparation for your first interview with a prospective employer which will have a positive influence on those you meet. Before leaving to go on an interview, be sure to check each of the items on this list:

- ☐ I am dressed in business attire, clean, freshly pressed and shined.
- ☐ I know exactly how to get to the meeting.
- ☐ I know how long it will take me to get there before the appointed time.
- ☐ I know the correct pronunciation of the name of the person to see.
- ☐ I have at least three clean copies of my resume.
- ☐ I have a notepad and a writing instrument.
- ☐ I have studied some company literature, and know what they make or do.
- ☐ I have cleared my calendar, so that I am not pressed for time.
- ☐ I know my resume extremely well, including dates and events.
- ☐ I am prepared to provide quantitative accomplishments for each job.
- ☐ I have studied the list of "tough" questions, and am prepared to answer them.
- ☐ I have a compensation range in mind that would meet my needs.
- ☐ I have a positive, "I can do" attitude; no chips on my shoulder today.

Another important area of influence that is often overlooked or ignored is the impact that you have on employees not in the direct line of interviewing. Receptionists and secretaries have been known to affect a hiring decision, especially when treated with lack of respect. Do not slight any of these people. Rather watch and observe, interact when appropriate, and be polite.

Attitude: Project a Positive Self-Image

Display a positive attitude during an interview. Do not make disparaging remarks about previous employers or supervisors. Do not carry a chip on your shoulder because you were terminated, didn't get a raise or for any other reason.

Self-confidence adds another positive dimension to your character. The interviewer wants to be assured that you feel confident about your capabilities and that you can handle the position. Don't give the impression that you are desperate for just any job.

Dare to Be Different

I have mentioned several times that cute doesn't do it. The green resume is an eye-catcher, but will not set you apart from the crowd for the right reasons.

Marketing gurus often talk about how a product is packaged to attract the right consumer. You also need to be packaged to be attractive to the employer. After reading your resume, or after you have left an interview, the impression must be positive. You need to set yourself apart from the crowd.

You may have read about people who did wild things to get their jobs. Literally camping on the door step of a company, wearing a sandwich board at a busy street corner intersection, sending a video resume to the home of the hiring manager, are just a few examples that may have worked. They may be different, but not what most hiring people would consider appropriate.

Be Different In a Professional Way!

#1. Construct a cover letter and resume that is clear, concise and demonstrates your accomplishments.

#2. Arrive for the interview in your best business attire.

#3. Be knowledgeable about the company and yourself.

#4. Know what you want, why you want it, and how to get there.

Tips for Success

- ► Visit a company prior to the interview. Pick up company literature and study in preparation for meetings. At the same time, observe employees: style and personalities.
- ► Know precisely all the details on your resume.
- ► Have ready at least ten quantitative accomplishments that are not listed on your resume.
- ► Present a positive, can-do, self-confident attitude, but do not forget your sense of humor.
- ► Focus totally on the interview—leave all excess baggage behind. You are there to get an offer of employment!

P A R T

6

Your Interview: Passing the Test

THE INTERVIEW PROCESS

The interview is your direct connection to a job offer. You have arrived at the Right Place, at the Right Time and, hopefully, with the Right Credentials. The obstacles that you must now overcome are "chemistry" with the people you will be working for and with, and competition from others who are seeking the same position. The previous section should have prepared you for what you now face—the interview.

Exercise: True or False

Test your knowledge of the interview process with the following:

	True	False
1. If asked to describe your weaknesses, just say that you do not have any.	☐	☐
2. Be sure to ask about the company benefits during the first interview.	☐	☐
3. Do not stretch the truth.	☐	☐
4. Take control of the interview early in the process.	☐	☐
5. If taken to lunch, relax; it is probably not part of the interview process.	☐	☐
6. Respond only to the questions asked; never volunteer anything.	☐	☐
7. If the interviewer asks an illegal question, point it out politely.	☐	☐
8. Take notes when asking questions about the company or job.	☐	☐
9. If the interview is during dinner, limit your alcoholic beverages to two.	☐	☐
10. Never tell an interviewer that you were terminated or fired from a job.	☐	☐

Answers
True: 3, 4, 8
False: 1, 2, 5, 6, 7, 9, 10

THE INTERVIEW PROCESS (continued)

An interview has several steps.

Step 1: After everyone is at ease, the process begins with you telling your story. This takes the form of your responding to questions by the interviewer, or your providing your life history.

Step 2: There may be some additional testing of your skills through problem solving, or discussions of real world, or company concerns.

Step 3: This is the exchange about the position and the company. The interviewer tries to sell you on the opportunity.

Step 4: The final step is the close.

Step 5: A company will invite a finalist candidate back for a second, and perhaps even a third round of interviews. Although you may feel more comfortable, do not let down your guard. Take the posture that you are still competing with others. You just made the first or second cut.

Phone Talk

An interview may start with a phone call. This may be only the first in a series of screenings, and will determine whether you should be interviewed in person. The phone interviewer will hit upon your career highlights to determine if you have the right credentials.

A phone interview can sometimes come out of nowhere. You were not responding to an ad, and you had not submitted a resume. You have had no chance to prepare for the interview. Your name was given to a company or recruiter by a third party. This is what you have been working toward through networking—a company is coming after you!

Be prepared for any call at any time, especially if you are actively in the job market. Have a copy of your resume and a pad and pencil near the phone. You can turn that surprise call to your advantage. The caller will often be selling you about an opportunity and a company. You can end up asking the questions!

A word of caution. Although you may think it is cute for your five-year-old to answer the phone, make it easier for the caller to get to you or leave a message. Job changes are serious business.

Another word of caution. Unanswered calls may lead to missed opportunities. You must have an answering machine in good working order. If a caller can not leave a message, you may never receive a call back.

Let's (*Not*) Talk Money

The phone interviewer will eventually get around to asking about your compensation requirements and history. If your compensation is too high for the position, the interviewer may assume that you would not be interested in the position, or that you are over-qualified. The employer may be reluctant to hire someone at a salary which is significantly lower than what they have been earning. The assumption is that the person may continue to look for a higher paid position after they have joined the firm.

If your compensation has been significantly lower than the compensation for the new position, the employer may question whether you are ready for a position at that higher level. It is tough to win if your compensation is either dramatically higher or lower than the position for which you are applying. However, there is a way to avoid this predicament.

Before the question of compensation is brought up by the interviewer, you should take the initiative. Ask the interviewer about the compensation: "Could you give me some indication of the compensation package?" This question should come after the interviewer has already discussed the position, and you have provided some of your credentials.

The interviewer may respond with the compensation range. You can then say that it certainly is within your consideration. This may end the discussion of compensation until a later time.

Try to delay providing your specific compensation data until the last possible moment. This will probably take place after you have had a personal interview. If you did a good job of selling yourself, you may be offered a salary at the high end of the salary range, or the company might develop a compensation package that is more attractive and acceptable.

THE INTERVIEW PROCESS (continued)

Compensation Negotiation

The best time to negotiate the most advantageous compensation package is when you join a company. When you get a job offer, you can be sure that the company feels that you will make a substantial contribution to their future. They want to insure that you will accept the offer. At that point it is not a question of if they want you, but how much it will cost to get you. You are finally in the driver's seat.

The company has a predetermined salary range. A position may include a bonus or some other form of incentive compensation. Do not be afraid to ask what the compensation range is for the position. In addition to your capabilities and previous compensation package, your attitude and self-confidence will have an effect on the offer.

There are many reasons to accept a position besides compensation, such as job satisfaction, the nature of the work, the location, the people you will be working with, the company's strength and future prospects, and the company benefits, such as stock options. But when it comes down to *your* bottom line, future compensation increases and bonus potentials are usually based on a percentage of your present compensation. Therefore, the level at which you start will set the base for your future earnings.

IN THE BEGINNING . . .

You have arrived for the interview. After the usual, ''Did you have any trouble finding us?'' or ''Can you believe this weather?'' the interview begins to take shape. The interview agenda can take two basic forms: a reverse chronological discussion, such as ''Tell me about your current position and work backward''; or chronologically from the beginning, probably starting with your education.

Generally, the interviewers that you will encounter (except for most human relations and employment personnel) will not be experienced interview professionals. They may themselves be anxious and intimidated by the interview process. This is another place where you can do yourself some good.

Try to make the interview less stressful for the interviewer! By doing this, you will develop a smoother rapport and ''chemistry.'' Good chemistry is likely to produce a positive impression, and has been known to have more influence on hiring decisions than the best of credentials.

To help make an interviewer more comfortable, consider the following actions.

Volunteer Information

Keep the discussion going with relevant information where you control the content and direction. Take control without pressing it.

Extol Your Accomplishments

This is not the time to be modest. However, avoid the ''I'' and ''me'' and impress teamwork. Then when you are asked who was specifically responsible for something, take the credit if it was you.

Avoid Confrontation

Do not take issue unless prompted to do so as part of the interview.

Exhibit Open Body Language

Lean into the conversation; keep your arms unfolded, smile, and use positive facial expressions, such as nodding with understanding.

IN THE BEGINNING . . . (continued)

Ask Questions

The following questions will demonstrate your seriousness about, and interest in the position, the company and your future. They should be asked of the person to whom you would report. You might reserve some of these questions until you are called back for a second interview:

- How will my job success be measured? Are there specific goals?
- How do you expect this position to affect your job?
- How do you visualize this position changing in the next two years?
- Where do you expect the company to be in two years?
- Describe your management style. How would we work together?
- How might this position benefit my career?
- Have any key players left within the last six months? Why?
- Why should someone with my background and experience want to join this company?

QUESTIONS THAT BEG ANSWERS

During the interview you may be asked some tough questions. Here are some that you should be prepared to answer:*

1. What have been the most serious problems that you've had with people who have worked for or with you? How have you resolved them?
2. Give five adjectives that generally describe the people who work for you.
3. What bores you about your present job?
4. If you had the opportunity to change anything in your work career, what would you have done differently?
5. Have you ever considered another career? If so, what?
6. What motivates you to be successful?
7. What kind of responsibilities would you like to avoid in your next job?
8. How do you feel about exaggerating or telling a white lie to sell a product? When should it be permissible?
9. Describe the importance of your current or most recent position within the company's overall business plan.
10. What specifically do you want to receive from your next job and company?
11. When checking references with your current or most recent supervisor, what would they feel have been your greatest accomplishments to the department and to the company?
12. What could have been different in your current or last employment that would have resulted in our not discussing job opportunities today?
13. If you had been in your supervisor's position, what would you have done differently in your department or group?
14. What personal criteria have you used to evaluate candidates for professional positions that have reported to you?
15. How far should you go in checking references on candidates for professional or managerial positions? Why?

*Source: *Hiring Winners,* Pinsker, AMACOM, 1991.

QUESTIONS THAT BEG ANSWERS (continued)

Practice answering these questions with someone who can and will give an honest critique and feedback. A colleague would probably be more appropriate than a close friend. Your answers should demonstrate:

- ✓ A positive attitude toward your career, employers and life
- ✓ A planned approach to your career
- ✓ Significant quantitative accomplishments that have contributed to an employer's objectives
- ✓ Adaptability and flexibility in working as a team player
- ✓ Competence in meeting the expectations of the position

How to Respond to an Illegal Question

An interviewer may err in asking a question that is considered illegal or discriminatory. For example, ''When did you graduate from high school?'' would reveal your age. ''Where did you grow up?'' could reveal your national origin.

You could: a) point this out to the interviewer; b) complain to some governmental body; or c) answer the question and carry on. If you have a real interest in the position and want to maintain rapport, the answer is ''c.'' Why ruffle feathers? You are there to get hired!

How to Handle Negative Information in the Interview

Negative information can take many forms. You may have had a series of short tenure (less than one year) positions. You may have been fired from a job. Your salary may be on the decline. Whatever the situation, how you handle it can make all the difference. Here are a few guidelines:

- **Develop a positive side of the issue.** What did you learn or gain from the situation? How do you plan on avoiding this situation in the future? Be prepared for what your references may say about the situation. You should ask your references how they will respond so that you will be prepared.

- **Volunteer the information, stressing the information above.** Employers do not like to get surprises when checking references. If negative information may come out during reference checking, then alert the interviewer. Timing can be everything.

  Sometimes negative information will come out during the natural course of the interview. Let it happen, but do not make a big point of it. Other times it may best be brought out after you have already sold the company on your strengths and their need to hire you.

- **Do not deny or react hostiley defensive.** Defend your actions and decisions with logic and reason. If you made a bad decision, acknowledge it. Arguing the point will get you nowhere.

  Here are some reasons for ''situations'':

  - I should have investigated the company more thoroughly before I joined.
  - I took a chance with a start-up; and it did not go anywhere.
  - I differed in philosophy with the president (or whomever).
  - My performance expectations were not clearly defined.
  - I gained some needed experience for my continued growth.
  - My boss, along with those he brought into the company, were all replaced.
  - A downsize, which I supported, resulted in my position being eliminated, along with several other key players.
  - Total compensation, which included equity, was more important to me than just a base salary.

THE CLOSE

A savvy candidate knows when to stop selling. If you need to continue selling your capabilities all the way to the door you may appear to be too anxious, or too concerned about how well you were received.

After you have finished the interview and shaken hands, stop selling. Instead, ask ''Could you give me some indication of your time table?'' Show that you are sensitive to the interviewer's agenda.

You can often judge an employer's interest at the end of your first interview by their closing line or action:

- A job offer is promised. Beware! It is too soon.
- They are interviewing others and will call. Okay.
- You are asked to provide references. Good!
- You are invited back for more interviews. Excellent!

The Breaking Bread Interview

You may be invited to be interviewed at a restaurant. The following suggestions are made based on real interview experiences with executives. Know how to handle these situations ahead of time. They are just plain common sense:

- Know and follow the basic manners of eating in public.
- Do not come to the meal ravenous because you probably will not be able to finish your meal.
- Do not order alcoholic beverages at breakfast or lunch.
- If your host orders alcohol at dinner, you may order wine, beer, or a non-alcoholic beverage. Remember to sip your drink.
- Take small bites, and never answer a question with food in your mouth.
- Do not order the most expensive item on the menu; stay in the middle of the price range.
- Do not offer to pick up the check; it is not expected.

AFTER THE INTERVIEW

Your "after interview" protocol must also be appropriate. The following guidelines should be useful:

1. Write a brief (three paragraphs maximum) letter addressed to the hiring manager expressing an interest in the position and re-emphasizing one of your strengths as it relates to a major position requirement. Your letter will require the hiring manager to take some action, like placing your letter with your file. Therefore, your file will once more be brought to the top of the pile.

The following is an example of a good after-interview letter:

January 2, 19XX

Ms. Alice M. Silvers
Vice President, Sales and Marketing
Advanced Widgits, Inc.
1234 Fifth Street
Anywhere, US 12345

Dear Ms. Silvers:

Thank you for your time in discussing the National Sales Manager opportunity with Advanced Widgits.

Based on the key responsibilities and performance goals you identified, my sales management experience and results with Hi-Tech Things indicate parallel expectations and achievements. Over the last five years, through the introduction of a new product line and the revitalization of the sales force, we achieved record sales increases of better than 22% per year. We also formulated a long-term strategic marketing plan, and succeeded in capturing a 30% market share during that same period.

I am excited about the opportunity with Advanced Widgits, and look forward to continuing our discussions.

Sincerely,

AFTER THE INTERVIEW (continued)

2. Do not phone to inquire about the status of the recruitment effort, where you stand among candidates, or when you will hear from them again. If you were referred by a recruitment firm, they will keep you posted.

3. Do phone the hiring manager if you truly have a conflict, like another job offer, and you need to know whether you are being considered for their position. This action can be a little tricky. You may be forcing an issue that they are not ready to respond to and thus may eliminate yourself from consideration. Only use this tactic if you really are in such a conflicting position.

Tips for Success

- Don't bring up the issue of compensation until you are forced to discuss it. The first person to mention a number loses the negotiation advantage.
- You may not get along with every interviewer. You might appear to be a threat to some people. However, it is your job to insure that the best chemistry occurs at every opportunity. Try to make their interview task easier.
- Read about interviewing and prepare for all types of questions. Make sure that interview events come as no surprise to you.
- Display your interest and excitement in the job and company, but be careful not to appear too anxious and hungry. *You can only turn down or accept an offer that you receive.*

P A R T

7

Endorsements: What Will They Say About You?

REFERENCES—YOU CAN BET YOUR CAREER ON THEM

An employer will check your references. Employers are expecting greater results with fewer employees today, so the importance of each new hire has become more crucial. Although the concern for litigation has resulted in many employers refusing to provide any information but the basics, assume that your references will be thoroughly checked. Therefore, *never exaggerate your capabilities, responsibilities, and accomplishments beyond reality.*

Keep this principle in mind while you are writing your resume, and during your interview discussions. Here are a few suggestions:

- Only claim degrees or certificates that can be verified.
- Do not exaggerate results such as sales or production figures that are more than 120% of reality.
- Do not take credit for actions or results that are not yours.
- Do not imply close business ties or relationships with people or companies when in fact they were casual or distant.

Who Will Serve as a Reference?

You will be asked to provide the names of subordinates, peers or supervisors to serve as references. Employers will put little or no value on any written reference letters which you provide—negative statements are never put into writing.

If you have been employed by the same company for several years, providing names from that company may be a cause for some concern, particularly if your job search is confidential. Consider using confidants that you have developed within the company, or people who have recently left. Perhaps others with whom you have had business relationships outside of the company, such as customers, might maintain your confidentiality, and still serve as good references.

An employer who does a thorough job of checking your references will go beyond the list which you provide. They may make use of informal industry and community networks to check you out. You may never even know to whom they talked about your performance.

The person who speaks with your references will assume that you have contacted the reference person and alerted them to expect a call. The caller will also assume that you have guided the reference person about what to say. So you might as well tell the reference person about the position, and what strengths would be appropriate for success.

WHAT QUESTIONS WILL BE ASKED?

Here are some examples of questions that will be asked of the people who serve as your references:*

- How and when did you know the candidate, and what was your relationship to the candidate?
- Trace the candidate's progress and relationship with you and the company.
- What were the candidate's most significant accomplishments? (They will want individual, specific results, not departmental accomplishments.)
- What were the major strengths you noted in the candidate?
- We all have some shortcomings or areas that can be improved upon. What were the candidate's shortcomings, and how did he or she accommodate them?
- Why did the candidate leave your company? Do you know why he or she might be thinking of leaving?
- How would you describe the candidate's relationships with others? (This includes peers, subordinates, customers and any others who might be appropriate.)
- We are considering the candidate for a position that involves (they will describe the position). From your experience working with the candidate, specifically where do you believe he or she would contribute to this position, and why do you feel that way?
- How would you describe the candidate's employment with your company, and where would you rank the candidate in comparison to others in similar positions?
- Would you want to work for or with this person again? In what kind of environment?
- Who else in your company should we talk to about the candidate?

---

*Source: *Hiring Winners,* Pinsker, AMACOM, 1991.

Exercise: Endorsement Review

To ensure that you have a realistic picture of your employment history, on a separate piece of paper, answer the questions honestly. If possible, have a trusted co-worker or associate answer these questions about you also. Compare answers and discuss any significant discrepancies.

Tips for Success

- Assume that *everything* you write or say will be verified. Therefore, control exaggeration—keep it to within the realities someone else will remember and report.
- *Never* say you have a college degree if it is not true.

P A R T

8

The Last Word

CONSULTING CAN LEAD TO EMPLOYMENT OPPORTUNITIES

Landing a consulting assignment may open the door to full-time employment. Here are some ways to make this happen:

- Always do a superior, professional consulting job.
- Try to work as part of the company team rather than as an independent contractor, unless that is why you were hired.
- Promote the value of your services to include the implementation of your recommendations.
- Be alert for follow-up work for which you are the best person to handle the task.
- Ask the client how and where you might fit into the organization.
- Let the client know that you would prefer full-time involvement as an employee of the company.
- Ask the client for recommendations to other companies.
- If you are considering consulting as a career, contact the Institute of Management Consultants at (212) 697-8262 for more information. The Institute has local small group meetings, as well as semi-annual regional and annual national conferences.

THE GETTING HIRED ACTION LIST

1. *Extol Your Accomplishments!*

   Only if your accomplishments are well recognized, will any employer beat a path to your door. Let the movers and shakers inside and outside your company know about your successes.

2. *Get Well Known!*

   Become active in organizations, particularly those related to your profession or career. Write articles, serve on committees, speak up at meetings and become recognized.

3. *Stretch the Truth But Not More Than 120%!*

   Never put in writing or take credit for results that can not be verified. Some stretch is expected because you are selling, but be careful of statements that might betray you.

4. *Ensure That Your Resume Will Be Read Thoroughly!*

   Your resume may only get 10 seconds. Design it as a marketing tool targeted to get an interview. Never more than two pages, it should be professionally designed and printed on fine white paper.

5. *Send Your Resume Only to a Decision Maker!*

   Always address your resume to a specifically named person, two levels above the position for which you are applying. Budgets and personnel changes flow downward in the organization.

6. *Send Each Resume With a Cover Letter!*

   Tailor the cover letter to meet the needs of the prospective employer. Tell how and what they will gain from hiring you; not what you expect from them.

7. *Assume You Are Always Being Interviewed!*

   Although it may appear to be just a friendly lunch, you are being judged for fit and capabilities. Get comfortable only after you are hired.

8. *Assume Your References Will Be Checked in Depth!*

   References from former employers and others will be checked, often by indirect methods. Employers have built strong networks to accomplish this. You can bet your career on it.

9. ***Be Moderate in Communicating with a Company or Search Firm!***

There is a fine line between establishing rapport and demonstrating enthusiasm for a position, and appearing overly anxious (bordering on obnoxious). Know when to stop selling.

10. ***Guide the Interview in the Direction You Want It to Take!***

A trained interviewer will discover how well you match the job. However, few managers are trained interviewers. You need to help them make that match through subtle control.

11. ***Know Your Career in Detail!***

Know who you are (strengths and shortcomings), when (dates) and where (organizations) you have been and specifically what you have accomplished (quantitatively or qualitatively). Demonstrate your ability to improve bottom-line results.

12. ***Network on an On-going Basis!***

Handle each meeting with a friend, colleague or prospective employer as if it could lead you to an exciting job opportunity. Maintain contacts with those you have met. Exchange job opportunity information with others. Keep your network of contacts alive.

13. ***Save Salary Discussions Until the End!***

Indicating current or recent compensation immediately places you in a salary range. If your pay is above what a company might offer, you might lose out on an important job opportunity. Should your pay be significantly lower than what a company might offer, they may feel you are not ready for that particular level of position.

KEEP YOUR ANTENNA TUNED

Throughout your career you will be exposed to many job opportunities.

✔ Explore All of Them Carefully

✔ Go On Interviews

✔ Meet New People

✔ Consider Each Person You Meet As a Lead to Other Opportunities

An interview can also lead to a job that is different from the job that caused you to have the interview in the first place. Your skills and experience might even cause the interviewer to create a new position for you.

Summary

► Successful job changes require a proactive approach; early and continued networking pays off.

► Preparation and knowledge go hand-in-hand, so know your accomplishments thoroughly, and learn about prospective employers before your first interview.

► Prepare for an interview like it was your "finals week"—it just may be a lot more important.

► Direct your total effort toward receiving a job offer. You can always turn it down, *but without a job offer you will never get hired.*

NOTES

NOTES

NOTES

NOTES

NOTES

NOTES

OVER 150 BOOKS AND 35 VIDEOS AVAILABLE IN THE 50-MINUTE SERIES